OXFORDSHIRE COUNTY COUNCIL
Woodeaton Manor School
Woodeaton
Oxford OX3 9TS
Telephone: Oxford 58722

TEAMWORK
Newspapers

Philippa Perry and Stephen Gibbs

Wayland

Reporter
Ernest Taylor
(pages 10–11)

Sub-editor
Lucy Bell
(pages 16–17)

Editor
Dan Mason
(pages 8–9)

Picture editor
Malcolm Hepple
(pages 12–13)

Photographer
George Archer
(pages 14–15)

Imprint details are on page 31.

Printer
Ron Robinson
(pages 26-7)

Production editor
Ray Walker
(pages 24-5)

Advertising manager
Liz Ashby
(pages 18-19)

Designer
Nick Wongsam
(pages 20-21)

Artist
Lisa Bridge
(pages 22-3)

Contents

Yesterday's News	4
The 'Press Gang'	6
The Editor	8
The Reporter	10
The Picture Editor	12
The Photographer	14
The Sub-Editor	16
The Advertising Manager	18
The Designer	20
The Artist	22
The Production Editor	24
The Printer	26
The Newspaper Seller	28
Glossary	30
Books to read	31
Index	32

Yesterday's News

Newspapers have been around since Roman times. The very earliest newspaper was called *Acta Diurna*, which means 'the daily news'. It was a handwritten news-sheet that was first pasted on to walls in Rome in 59 BC. It told people about the latest army battles and political events. Readers could even check up on the results of gladiator fights.

'Hear Ye!'
During the Middle Ages very few people could read. Instead, they heard the news from travellers. Actors and singers, called troubadours, went all over the country telling people the news. Some towns had their own town criers who would ring a bell and announce the news twice a day.

▲ In the past town criers rang a bell and announced the news to the public.

▲ Disasters and tragedies make headline news.

Fact-file
- The River Fleet was finally bricked up when a butcher accidentally fell into it and died.
- Before the printing press was invented in the 1440s, newspapers used to be written out by hand.
- The number of copies of a newspaper sold every day is called its circulation. With 5 million copies sold every week, *The News of the World* is the highest-circulation newspaper in Britain.

Fleet Street

For about 300 years, Fleet Street in London was the centre of Britain's newspaper industry. Wynkyn de Worde was the first person to print a newspaper there. In those days it wasn't really a street at all but a muddy, smelly river called the River Fleet. But it was close to the City of London, which was the main business area of the capital. Wynkyn de Worde was able to sell his paper to the lawyers and merchants who worked there. Before long, other newspaper publishers moved into the area.

Race against time

In the great days of Fleet Street, printing newspapers was a slow, fiddly business. All the pages were laid out by hand. Each letter was carved on a small metal block and the printer would carefully position each letter to form the words of the news reports and headlines. Today pages of news can be written and designed on computer screens and printed at the touch of a button.

▲ Newspaper pages used to be laid out by hand. Now, newspapers are produced using computers.

This early printing press is being used to produce a news-sheet. Before the 1440s, books and news-sheets had to be copied out by hand. ▶

The 'Press Gang'

Every day 29 million people in Britain read a daily newspaper. Have you ever wondered just what goes into producing your 'daily'? It takes a lot of hard work with everyone on the team having an important part to play. Without teamwork your newspaper would never get to your breakfast table on time.

There are many different kinds of newspapers; daily, evening, weekly, national and local. They usually come in two different sizes, broadsheet or tabloid.

On a national newspaper there may be as many as 2,000 people, all working together to get their paper to homes and news-stands on time. But however big or small, producing a newspaper involves one important thing: teamwork.

The *Coventry Evening Telegraph*

The *Coventry Evening Telegraph* has a circulation of 64,000 copies every day, which means that it is one of the highest-circulation evening newspapers outside London. In this book we will see how the team at the *Coventry Evening Telegraph* work together to produce its newspaper.

This is the team at the *Coventry Evening Telegraph*. Find out more about their jobs and how they work together on the relevant pages of this book. ▶

The News of the World is the highest-circulation newspaper in Britain. ▼

**Photographer
George Archer**
(pages 14 – 15)

**Picture editor
Malcolm Hepple**
(pages 12 – 13)

Sub-editor – Lucy Bell
(pages 16 – 17)

Reporter – Ernest Taylor
(pages 10 – 11)

**Editor
Dan Mason**
(pages 8 – 9)

**Designer
Nick Wongsam**
(pages 20 – 21)

Newspaper seller
(pages 28 – 9)

Artist – Lisa Bridge
(pages 22 – 3)

Printer – Ron Robinson
(pages 26 – 7)

**Production editor
Ray Walker**
(pages 24 – 5)

**Advertising manager
Liz Ashby**
(pages 18 – 19)

The Editor

The editor is in charge of the whole team. It is his or her job to decide which stories will go into the newspaper every day. In order to make sure that the newspaper is interesting so that people want to buy it, the editor needs to know what kind of stories the readers like to see reported.

The editor's day

The editor's day begins with a meeting with all the chief editors from each department to discuss the news, reports and features that could be printed in the next day's newspaper. If the team are not sure which stories to use, the editor always makes the final decision.

> **Dan Mason**
> 'The most exciting thing is when a big story breaks just before the final deadline and we hold the paper for it. Then everyone has to work on the story together as a team to bring it all together.'

▲ Every day the editor discusses the day's news with the chief editors of each department, sub-editors and reporters.

The editor gets reports throughout the morning from each department on how the stories are going. As soon as each page is ready, the editor looks at it and makes sure everything is running on time. The editor always sees the full paper just before the final deadline. After the paper has 'gone to bed' (been sent to be printed), the editor starts to plan for the following day's edition, deciding which reporters should cover which stories.

▲ Dan Mason is the editor of the *Coventry Evening Telegraph*.

The artist is showing the editor an illustration for a feature on Christmas shopping. ▶

Fact-file

- If there is an important story, such as the general election results, the editor asks the whole team to work through the night so that the reports are up-to-date.
- The editor answers all the letters that are sent in by the newspaper's readers. The editor uses the best ones on the letters page.
- Each edition of a major national newspaper such as *The Times* contains as many words as there are in three full-size novels. Phew!

The Reporter

It is the job of the newspaper reporter to find and write the news stories which will appear in the next day's paper. Every day, the editor gives each reporter a number of stories to follow up and write about. Some of the time the reporter is out of the office, interviewing members of the public.

A good reporter will know lots of people who work in certain jobs or are experts on a subject. If the reporter needs advice about a particular story, or would like to use a quotation to help explain something in the report, he or she will telephone them for help. These people are sometimes called 'contacts'.

▲ Reporters spend a lot of time on the telephone following up reports.

Ernest is taking notes while talking to a witness. ▼

Ernest Taylor
" Being a reporter is a very stressful job – that's the best thing about it. You've got to write a good story by the deadline and that can be very exciting. "

Following up a story

8.00 a.m. The reporter arrives at the office.
8.10 a.m. The telephone rings. Somebody has reported that a lion has escaped from the local zoo.
8.15 a.m. The reporter mentions the story to the editor.
9.00 a.m. The story is discussed at the morning meeting. The editor decides to use it as the paper's main story for that day.
9.15 a.m. The reporter rushes out to interview the zoo keeper, witnesses and the police.
10.30 a.m. Back in the office, starts to write up the story on his or her computer.
11.00 a.m. Shows the story to the editor who says that it is fine but needs a quotation from an animal expert.
11.15 a.m. Telephones the local university and talks to Dr Heart, the lion expert.
11.59 a.m. Finishes writing the story one minute before the 12.00 p.m. deadline.
12.00 – 5.00 p.m. Starts to think about stories for the following day's edition.

Fact-file

- Reporters call the stories they write their 'copy'.
- All reporters want to get their own 'scoop'. This is when they are first to report an important story.
- Not every story that a reporter writes gets printed. Some get 'spiked', or dropped, when the editor feels they're not interesting enough.

◀ Ernest is writing up the 'copy' of his report on his computer. He is checking his notes and facts carefully so that the report is correct.

The Picture Editor

Newspapers are not just made up of words – the pictures are very important as well. It is the picture editor's job to choose which pictures to use in the newspaper.

Every day the picture editor goes to the morning meeting with the rest of the team. Together with the editor and the reporter, the picture editor decides which stories will need a photograph to go with them.

The picture editor is in charge of all the photographers. He or she decides which photographer to send on which story and keeps track of where the photographers are due to go in a special diary.

▲ The picture editor, Malcolm Hepple, chooses which photographs are used in the newspaper.

Malcolm Hepple
❝ I rely on my photographers to come up with interesting photographs. Then, I can choose the one that will give a story even more impact. ❞

▲ The picture editor meets with the photographer to discuss what kind of photograph is needed for a report.

12

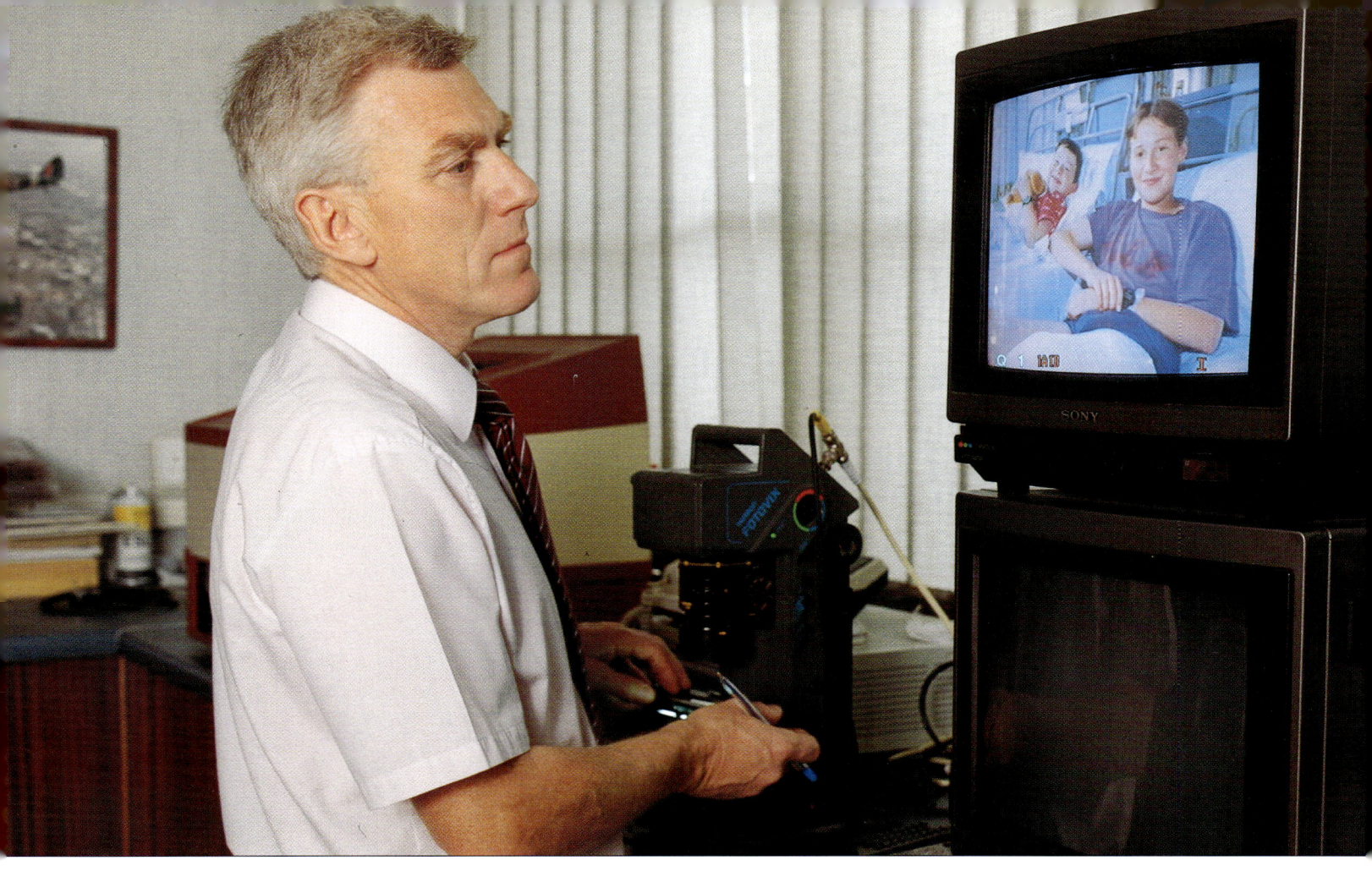

When a photographer returns with some photographs on film the picture editor checks the film on a special machine, called a photograph scanner. This machine enlarges the photographs so that the picture editor can choose the best one. The best photograph is then printed and passed on to the sub-editor (see pages 16–17).

▲ **The picture editor checking a photograph on the photograph scanner. He is making sure that the picture is sharp and clear so that it will look good in the newspaper.**

Fact-file
- All pictures are kept on file in the newspaper's own picture library in case the picture editor wants to use them again.
- A picture story is one based around a really good photograph.
- If you look closely at a newspaper photograph you will see that it is printed in thousands of tiny dots which make up the picture.

The Photographer

The photographer takes the pictures that will be used in the newspaper. He or she has to make sure that the photographs are eye-catching and interesting so that people want to buy the newspaper when they see it on the news-stand.

'A picture says a thousand words'
8.30 a.m. The photographer arrives at the newspaper and checks the camera bag contains all the equipment and film needed.
9.00 a.m. The picture editor gives the photographer the day's jobs, or assignments.

Photographers often have to rush out to jobs and always have their cameras ready. ▶

▲ Before he sets off on an assignment, the photographer checks that all his camera equipment is working properly.

9.15 a.m. The photographer discusses with the picture editor what each photograph should look like and whether he or she should use black and white or colour film.

The photographer is told when he or she must be back at the newspaper office so that the picture can be developed and printed in time for the deadline.

10.00 a.m. The first assignment is to photograph the opening of a new shopping centre.

11.00 a.m. Back to the office with the film.

11.15 a.m. Out again, this time to photograph the local zoo keeper mentioned in the story about an escaped lion.

11.40 a.m. Sends the film back to the newspaper by motor-bike messenger, in time for the 12.00 p.m. deadline.

2.00 p.m. The picture editor sends the photographer out again to take pictures of a special event, such as children from a local school receiving prizes, that will appear in the newspaper later in the week.

5.00 p.m. Back to the office with the film to be printed and kept in the picture library until it is needed.

George Archer

' To be a good photographer, you have to be good with people. Many people get nervous when they are being photographed. The secret is to make them relax. '

Fact-file

- Newspapers will sometimes pay tens of thousands of pounds just for one special or unusual photograph.
- A photographer can use up to ten reels of film just to get the one photograph that will be used in the newspaper.

The Sub-Editor

The sub-editor turns the reporter's copy into the story you read in the newspaper. Sometimes this involves lots of changes.

The sub-editor's day

The moment the reporter finishes his or her story, it is passed to the sub-editor, who is nicknamed the 'sub'. First the sub has to check the copy very carefully for any spelling mistakes or facts that may be wrong. Then the length of a story may have to be changed so that it fits on the page. Cutting a story from 5,000 to 500 words is a tricky job!

◀ The sub-editor, Lucy Bell, checks the reporters' copy.

The sub-editor also writes the captions, or words, that will go with the photographs. ▶

> **Lucy Bell**
> ❛ Thinking up good headlines is quite difficult. They have to grab the reader's attention – so they should be short but still explain what the story is about. ❜

◀ The sub-editor checks where the photographs and words will be positioned on the page. This helps her to know how long the report and headline should be.

The sub-editor usually explains to the reporter why the copy was changed to make sure there are no hard feelings!

Finally the sub-editor writes the headline for each story. These have to be eye-catching to make people buy the newspaper and encourage the readers to read on. This job is very important, as everybody knows that it is the headlines that sell newspapers.

Fact-file
- The most important part of any newspaper story is the first paragraph; sub-editors call this the 'nose' of the story.
- Modern computers make the sub-editor's job much easier. They can check spelling, move whole paragraphs and show where the picture will fit.

The Advertising Manager

▲ The advertising manager has to make sure that all the advertising space in the newspaper is sold.

◀ Advertising sales people spend a lot of their time talking to clients on the telephone.

Liz Ashby
"I enjoy talking to people all day and making sure all my clients' advertisements look good in the paper."

Most newspapers include advertising. Companies such as car manufacturers or shops buy space on a page of the newspaper to tell people about the things they want to sell. It is the job of the advertising manager and the sales team to sell this space.

Every day the advertising manager spends many hours on the telephone, ringing different companies to see if they want to advertise in the newspaper. The companies can buy any space from the tiniest square to a full-page, colour advertisement.

Front- and back-page advertisements are the most expensive because more people will see them.

When a space has been sold, the advertising manager sends down a copy of what the advertisement should say to the design department to design the advertisement.

It is not just companies that advertise in newspapers. Readers can also use the classified advertisement section of the paper to advertise to buy or sell almost anything. The newspaper charges for every word printed, so people try to keep their classified advertisements as short as possible.

The advertising team meet every day to check that all the advertisements in the paper look good. ▼

Fact-file
- Most of the cost of producing a newspaper is paid for by advertisers. Without advertisements your daily newspaper would cost three times as much.

The Designer

Designing the page
Every page on a newspaper is carefully laid out so that it looks as attractive as possible. This is the job of the designer.

As soon as a sub-editor has finished checking a story on the computer it is sent over to the designer's computer. The picture editor does the same with photographs. The designer then decides where each story and picture will go on each page.

▲ To make sure that the newspaper looks as attractive as possible, the designer discusses with the sub-editor how each page should be laid out.

By using a computer the designer can move pictures and words around at the touch of a button. When the page is completed the designer passes it to the editor to give it a final check before it goes to be printed.

▲ The designer, Nick Wongsam, uses his computer to lay out pages of advertisements.

Fact-file
- People read a page from top to bottom, so the most important stories always go at the top of a page.
- The words on newspaper pages are always printed in columns because they look neater and are easier to read.

Nick Wongsam
‘Being a designer on a newspaper you have to work very quickly and accurately. The job is never boring.’

◀ The designer is showing the advertising manager his ideas for an advertisement for one of her clients.

21

The Artist

▲ The artist, Lisa Bridge, is putting the final touches to an illustration.

Most newspapers have at least one artist on the team. The artist usually works in the design department. When an advertisement or a special feature needs to be illustrated with artwork, the designer tells the artist what sort of illustration is needed. The artist will then draw a rough pencilled drawing to show the designer and editor before going ahead with the finished version.

Lisa Bridge
❛ I love working as an artist for a newspaper. Every job is different, so I never get bored. ❜

The cartoonist

Cartoons are one of the most popular parts of a newspaper – some people buy their paper just for the cartoons. In some newspapers the artist in the design department draws the cartoons. After the morning editorial meeting, the artist discusses with the editor which story a cartoon could be based around. The artist then sketches some ideas.

When the editor has decided which idea is the best, the artist draws a pencilled outline of the cartoon. Then, he or she goes over this with a special ink-pen or felt-tip. Finally, the finished cartoon is shown to the editor before it goes to be printed.

The artist is going over a rough pencil outline of a cartoon of Father Christmas in ink-pen. ▼

Fact-file
- Newspaper artists have to work very fast. Sometimes they have only about two hours to come up with an idea and finish the drawing before the deadline.
- The most widely published newspaper cartoon strip is *Peanuts* with Charlie Brown and the gang. *Peanuts* cartoons have appeared in more than 2,000 newspapers in sixty-eight countries and twenty-six different languages since 1950.

The Production Editor

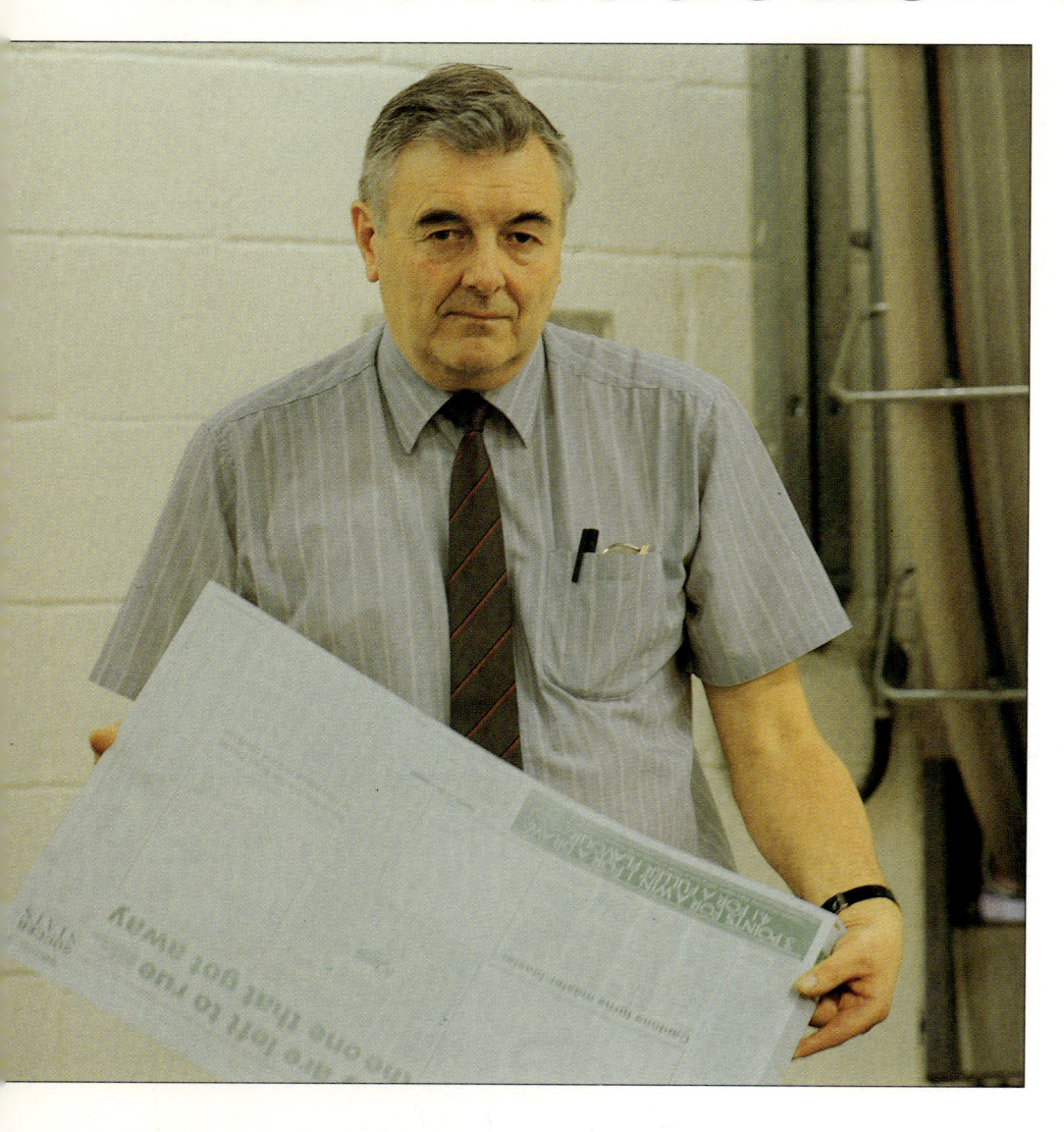

◄ The production editor, Ray Walker, checks each printing plate. The film of the pages and the printing plates can be damaged by ordinary office lighting so the production department is lit with yellow lights.

The production editor is in charge of the process of printing the newspaper. He or she has to make sure that the finished newspapers get to the readers on time.

Producing a newspaper

When the designer has laid out each page of the newspaper, a copy is printed out. This is photographed by a special machine. Each sheet of film for each page is then sent to the production department.

> **Ray Walker**
> ❝ I have to check each printing plate very carefully. If there is damage it will show up on the printed page. ❞

The production editor checks the film on a light-box for scratches or other damage. Then, the film is put into a special machine called a plate-maker and each sheet is copied on to an aluminium printing plate, which goes on the printing press.

Each day, the newspaper may be a different length, or have colour on different pages. The production editor has to make sure that the printing room is ready for the different needs of each day's edition.

When all the printing plates for the paper have been checked by the production editor they are handed over to the printer to put on to the press. Once this is done, the production editor orders the printer to start up the press.

Fact-file

- Any unused newsprint is sold as wrapping paper to fish and chip shops.

◀ **The production editor checks the special marks on the printing plates are in the right position so that they can be placed correctly on the printing press.**

The Printer

Go into the printing room of a modern newspaper and the first thing you will notice is how few people are around. Today, computers and machines do most of the work that was once done by hand by a whole team of printers.

But even the most modern machines cannot be left to operate on their own. The printer loads the huge rolls of newsprint on to the press, checks the different inks, fits the aluminium printing plates and checks the finished newspaper for printing and colour quality as it comes 'hot off the press'.

▲ The printer, Ron Robinson, has to check the information on his computer control screen before operating the press.

The printing process:

1. Each page is laid out on a computer screen.

2. The page is photographed and then turned into an aluminium printing plate.

3. A special plate-bending machine curves the plate to fit the press. As soon as the first plates are in position, the presses start rolling.

4. The plates never actually touch the paper. Instead they print on to a special rubber roller that passes over the paper. This process is called off-set printing.

5. As the newspapers come off the press they are folded automatically.

6. Conveyor belts take bundles of papers directly to the delivery vans, which are ready to take them to newsagents' shops and news-stands.

◀ The printer collects a copy of the newspaper from the press and checks that the colours are correct. He has copies of all the photographs used in the newspaper laid out beside him to check that they have been printed correctly.

▲ The printer snatches a copy from the conveyor belt to check the newspaper again before sending the newspapers off the press to be folded.

Ron Robinson
❝ It's my job to make sure the presses roll without a hitch. ❞

Fact-file

- Each newspaper travels at around 70 kilometres an hour around the press.
- The press costs over £3 million.
- A modern press can print about 60,000 newspapers an hour.

The Newspaper Seller

As soon as the newspapers roll off the presses, they are loaded into vans to be taken to newsagents and newspaper sellers. The newspaper seller sets up a news-stand on a street corner to sell to passers-by. He or she calls out the name of the paper to get people's attention.

As well as the bundles of papers, the newspaper seller is given a bill-board with the day's headlines for the big news stories written on it.

Fact-file
- If a newspaper seller sells a paper for 45p, he or she can keep 5p – the rest goes back to the newspaper publishers. So, the more papers the seller sells then the more money he or she earns.
- Some evening newspapers, such as the *Coventry Evening Telegraph* and *London Evening Standard*, sell most of their papers through newspaper sellers working on news-stands.

'I'm always counting on the team back at the office to come up with the best stories. Then I'll have no problem selling the papers.'

▶ The whole team inside the newspaper office has worked together to produce the newspaper on time.

EVENING TELEGRAPH
EVENING TELEGRAPH
Evening Telegraph
CITY HOSPITALS HIT BACK OVER LEAGUE TABLES
Evening Telegraph
CITY BOY STRANDED BY BUS DRIVER
YOUR BEST-EVER VALUE

Glossary

assignments The jobs that reporters or photographers are sent to work on by the editor.
bill-board The sign put in front of a news-stand on which the day's headline is written.
broadsheet A newspaper which is printed on large sheets of newsprint measuring 38 centimetres by 61 centimetres.
circulation The number of copies of a newspaper sold every day.
classified advertisements The short advertisements placed in a newspaper by the readers.
'contacts' Useful people that a reporter can get in touch with for help or advice on a story.
conveyor belts Fabric or metal plates moved by rollers which transport objects from one area to another.
'copy' Another word for the story that a reporter writes.
deadline The final time when work on a newspaper must be finished.
features Sections of a newspaper written about a particular subject of general interest which is not news.
headline The title of a newspaper story.
light-box A lighted box on which the picture editor or production editor lays film to check.

newsagents' shops Shops where newspapers are sold.
news-stands Movable stalls where newspapers are sold on the street.
newsprint The name for the special type of paper used for newspapers.
'nose' The first paragraph of a newspaper story.
off-set printing A type of printing where the plates do not touch the paper.
picture library A place where a newspaper's photographs are kept.
picture story A story that is based around an interesting or funny photograph.
'scoop' When a reporter is the first to discover a big story.
space The area on a newspaper page that is used for printing advertisements.
'spiked' The term used when a reporter's story is not used in the newspaper.
'sub' The nickname for a sub-editor.
tabloid A newspaper printed on newsprint sheets which measure 30 centimetres by 40 centimetres.
town criers People who announce local news or events to the public.
troubadours The name for travelling actors or singers who entertained the public and carried news from town to town in the Middle Ages.

Books to read

Breakthrough Communications By Philip Sauvah (Simon and Schuster, 1992)

Getting the Story – how the news is gathered by Libby Purves (Puffin, 1993)

Newspapers by Nancy Butler (Hodder and Stoughton, 1989)

Newspapers by Susannah Foreman (Heinemann, 1990)

Newspaper by John Price (Macmillan, 1991)

Useful Addresses

Newspapers Publishers Association
6 Bouverie Street
London
EC4Y 8AY

Newspaper Society
Whitefriars House
6 Carmelite Street
London
EC4 2BY

National Council for the Training of Journalists
Carlton House
Hemnall Street
Epping
Essex
CM16

Titles in the series
Building Site
Fire Service
Hospital
Newspapers
Police Service
Post Office

Series Editor: Geraldine Purcell
Series Designer: Loraine Hayes
© Copyright 1994 Wayland (Publishers) Limited

First published in 1994 by Wayland (Publishers) Limited
61 Western Road, Hove, East Sussex
BN3 1JD, England.

British Library Cataloguing in Publication Data

Perry, Philippa
Newspapers. - (Teamwork Series)
1. Title 11. Gibbs, Stephen 111. Series
070.1

ISBN 0 7502 1103 2

DTP Design by Loraine Hayes
Printed and bound in Italy by Rotolito Lombarda S.p.A.

Index

Acta Diurna 4
advertising manager 7, 18-19
artist 7, 22-3
assignments 14, 15, 30

bill-board 28, 30
broadsheet 6, 25, 30

cartoonist 23
circulation 4, 6, 30
classified advertisements 18
'contacts' 10, 30
Coventry Evening Telegraph, the 6, 28

design department 20-21, 22
designer 7, 20-21
de Worde, Wynkyn 5

editor 7, 8-9

features 8, 22, 30
Fleet Street 5

headlines 17, 28, 30

interviewing 10

letters page 9
light-box 25, 30
London Evening Standard, the 28

motor-bike messengers 15

News of the World, The 4, 6
newspaper sellers 7, 28

off-set printing 27, 30

photograph scanner 13
photographer 7, 12, 14-15
picture editor 7, 12-13, 14, 15

picture library 13, 30
plate-maker 25
printer 7, 26-7
printing plate 25, 26-7
printing press 25-7
production editor 7, 24-5

reporter 7, 10-11, 16
reports 8, 10-11, 16-17

'scoop' 11, 30
sub-editor 7, 13, 16-17, 20

tabloid 6, 30
Times, The 9
town criers 4, 30
troubadours 4, 30

Acknowledgements
The authors and publisher would like to thank the management and staff at the *Coventry Evening Telegraph* who co-operated in the making of this book.

Picture acknowledgements
All the photographs in this book were provided by Andrew Perris, APM Studios, except for the following: John Frost Historical Newspapers 4 (bottom), 6; Mary Evans Picture Library 4 (top); Topham Picture Library 5 (top); Wayland Picture Library 5 (bottom).